Spiritual

Spring Cleaning

by Debbie Schmid

Copyright © 1995 by Debra L. Schmid. Published by 21st Century Christian, 2809 Granny White Pike, Nashville, TN 37204.

ISBN #0-89098-144-2

Table of Contents

Section One: Light and Breezy

Section Two: Heavy Duty

Section Three: Finishing Touches

Appendix

Dedication

I dedicate this book to Sharon, my dear friend and sister in Christ. Thank you for "Spring Cleaning" with me! I enjoyed the many hours we spent together working through these lessons, and I deeply appreciate all your love, support, and encouragement.

Dear heavenly Father,

May each person who works through the pages of this book with You find renewed strength, hope, healing, and encouragement.

In Jesus' name I pray, amen.

Acknowledgments

Many thanks to Lois Knutson and Karen Pope for editing this manuscript, and to Betty Menke for help in typing. Your time and talents were greatly appreciated.

I also want to thank my "prayer warriors." This project would be incomplete without the cement of prayer. The Lord is so quick to listen to His children.

And to Tom and Kylea, a special thank-you for your patience with me when my time with you was spread thin in order to complete this book for the Lord. I appreciate your love and support.

Section One

Light and Breezy

Chapter One

The Pressure Cooker

"Oh, Tyler!" Angie grumbled angrily. "Can't you make it through one meal without spilling your milk?" She took a hurried swipe with the dish cloth as she ran to answer the phone. "I can see it's going to be another one of those days...and it's only eight o'clock!"

Angie picked up the receiver. "Hello," she said in her sweetest, most cheerful voice. "How are you today?...Us? Oh, we're great!...Why, yes, I'd be honored to serve on the new committee. I don't see any reason why I can't. Thank you for calling. Bye now."

Angie slammed down the receiver, grabbed the dish cloth, and knelt to wipe the spilled milk off the floor. "Can you believe it?" she snapped, looking at her husband, Mark. "Julie wants me to serve on another committee. Doesn't she know I'm already too busy? I wish they would find someone else for a change."

Mark sat quietly sipping his coffee and reading the morning newspaper. Lowering the paper, he peered at his wife. "Honey, if you're too busy, just say no. Don't make a big deal out of it. It's not that important."

"Say no?" Angie questioned in shock.

"Sure," he replied. "Don't feel obligated to be involved in every activity that comes your way."

"Oh, I don't know," Angie sighed. "It's just not my nature to say no."

"Yes, I know." Mark echoed her sigh.

"Besides, it sounds like a wonderful program," Angie continued.

"Hmmm. Aren't they all?"

Angie turned to her daughter. "Jenny, did you find your lost shoe yet?"

"No, Mommy," she wailed. "I've looked everywhere. Can you help me?"

"Can't you see I'm busy wiping up spilled milk? Keep looking! It's got to be around here somewhere." Angie glanced out the window only to notice the school bus driving past their house. "Oh great, Jenny! You missed the bus again! Why can't you be more organized? I'm tired of driving you to school every day on account of your carelessness."

Angie turned again and spoke to her husband. "That child!" she grumbled. "Jenny is so irresponsible. Sometimes she makes me furious!" Angie raised her voice once again at Jenny. "Hurry up! I'm going to be late for my meeting!"

Mark stood up, placed the newspaper on the table, finished drinking his coffee, and looked Angie in the eyes. "Honey, calm down. Perhaps you need to evaluate your priorities."

"What?!" She glared at him in disbelief. "*My* priorities are in order! What have *you* done this morning to help out?"

"Behind that newspaper, I prayed for you. It's what you needed most." He kissed Angie on the forehead and whispered, "I love you, 'Pressure Cooker.' I'll be home at six o'clock."

Mark met tearful Jenny in the hallway with the lost shoe in her hand. "Daddy, will you help me? Please?"

Mark tied her shoes and said, "Come on, Jenny. I'll take you to school this morning on my way to work so that Mommy can get to her meeting on time." Jenny scooted quickly out the door, never stopping to hug her mother or say good-bye. Angie watched from the front window as they got into the car and drove away. She brushed the tears from her cheeks and thought quietly to herself, "Priorities...pressure cooker...."

Angie returned to the kitchen and gently lifted screaming Tyler out of the high chair. "Don't cry, my precious little son. Everything is going to be okay."

Then she picked up the telephone receiver and dialed. "Pam, I'm calling to let you know I won't be at the meeting this morning after all."

"Is everything okay, Angie?" Pam asked.

"Yes, everything is fine. I just have something more important to take care of today. I'll call you later in the week." She gently replaced the receiver and comforted her sobbing son.

Dear heavenly Father,

Please help me put my priorities in the proper order and let my actions be proof of their importance.

In Jesus' name, amen.

Memory verse: Deuteronomy 6:5

Love the Lord your God with all your heart and with all your soul and with all your strength.

1. What are the main trouble spots in this story? (Example: Angie is too busy.)

2. What could Angie have done to help ease the tension in her home that morning?

3. Do you ever feel like a "pressure cooker"? If so, how often?

4. Does busyness affect your personality like it did Angie's? If yes, in what ways?

5. What could you do to change that?

6. Reflect back to a situation in your life that was similar to Angie's. How did you respond?

7. Were you happy with your actions? If not, what could you have done differently to ease the tension and change the situation?

8. Examine your upcoming calendar of events. Are you comfortably busy, or do you feel pressured and overloaded with things to do? If you are too busy, what specifically will you do to "unload" some of that extra weight?

9. List your priorities in order.

READ: Deuteronomy 6:5; 10:12, 13; 11:1; and Joshua 22:5.
10. According to these verses, how should we love the Lord?

11. What else should we do besides love the Lord? Give references.

12. Where is the Lord on your priority list? If He is not where He belongs, what will you do to change that?

READ: Proverbs 31:27.
13. Family members generally tend to rate high on our list of priorities. What does this woman do to show that her family is important to her?

14. What specific action does she avoid?

15. Do you think that since this woman "does not eat the bread of idleness" she is over-busy? Explain your answer.

16. How often do your actions match your priority list? If you are not satisfied with your actions, or if they do not match your priority list, what will you do to change that?

READ: Luke 10:38-40.
17. Explain how you are similar to Martha and/or Mary.

18. If Jesus came in the flesh to visit you today, what do you think He would say to you concerning your schedule?

19. There will always be times when life gets too busy and tensions mount. What can you do to help these situations go more smoothly?

20. When you feel too busy and stressed out, do you pray and ask the Lord to help you?

21. Are you afraid to say no, even when you know that your schedule is too full already? If so, is this fair to you or your family?

SPIRITUAL CHALLENGE: If someone asks you to do something and you already feel stressed out, or if you really don't want to do it for whatever reason, say no. Don't feel obligated to overload yourself. Simply respond gently and don't feel guilty about it.

You are special to the Lord and to others. Sometimes when we wear ourselves down too much, it affects those we love and care about the most. Be careful and enjoy the quiet blessings God has to offer.

Chapter Two

Silence

It was eight o'clock in the morning. Lisa arrived home after taking her youngest child to preschool. The house was quiet and Lisa felt at peace. Everyone had reached their destinations that morning, relaxed and on time.

The beds were made, and the dishwasher was running. Overall, the house was tidy. Lisa stood next to the counter and glanced at her calendar and a list of daily chores. She was instantly reminded of the busy schedule ahead. In the corner, she noticed the pile of mending and ironing. There was no end to her responsibilities as a mother and wife—yet Lisa had no question in her mind as to what came next.

Lisa poured herself a cup of hot tea and sat down at the kitchen table with her Bible and prayer journal. Nothing on her list was more important than Lisa's special time with her Lord.

Just as Lisa was about to pray, the telephone rang. "Should I answer it?" she wondered. "Of course I should. Perhaps one of my children is hurt or sick. Maybe my husband was in a car accident." Lisa's heart raced as she hurried to answer the phone.

"Hello," she said. Her best friend Shelly was on the other end of the line.

"Did I catch you at a bad time?" Shelly asked.

"Well, to be honest with you," Lisa answered, "I was just sitting down to study my Bible and pray. Are you calling from work?"

"No," Shelly replied. "I decided to take the day off so that I could catch up on some things at home."

"What are your plans for this afternoon?" Lisa asked. "Would it be convenient for you to meet me for an ice cream cone at about two o'clock? I have about forty-five minutes between my doctor's appointment and the time I need to pick the children up at school."

"That sounds like a great idea! I'm sure I'll be ready for a break by then," Shelly replied. "I'll look forward to seeing you at about two o'clock."

"Take care and thanks for calling. Bye."

Lisa hung up the telephone and eagerly went back to her special time with the Lord. After praying and reading the Bible, Lisa thought back to the days, not long ago, when time with the Lord came last in her day, if at all. She vividly remembered when her life and family members were stressed continually due to disorganization. Now that she had made the Lord top priority in her life, everything else fell into place. Lisa spent a lot of time getting organized and concentrated hard on keeping her priorities in order. As a result, Lisa's husband was happier, their children were happier, and Lisa was happier. Together they were drawing closer to the Lord and building close relationships with each other. The Lord blessed in many ways over and above what Lisa had set out to accomplish, and now she had the necessary strength to be a better wife and mother.

Dear heavenly Father,

It is in putting You first that I can glorify You and serve others best. Thank You for always being there for me and for helping me to put my priorities in the proper order. Help me to reserve a special time with You each and every day.

In Jesus' name I pray, amen.

Memory verse: Colossians 4:2
Continue earnestly in prayer, being vigilant in it with thanksgiving.

Daily prayer and Bible study keeps us close to our heavenly Father and provides us with the strength we need to face everyday trials and temptations.

1. Next to each verse, write when we should pray.

1 Chronicles 16:11

Ephesians 6:18

2. Why should we pray?

Matthew 26:41

Luke 22:40

3. Under what circumstances should we pray?

James 5:13-16

4. How often should we pray?

1 Thessalonians 5:17

5. Where should we pray?

Matthew 6:6

Acts 21:5

6. Does the Lord really hear our prayers?

Mark 11:24

1 John 3:22

7. Whose prayers does the Lord hear?

John 9:31

1 Peter 3:12

8. For whom does the Lord want us to pray?

Matthew 5:44

Luke 6:28

James 5:16

9. For what does the Lord want us to pray?

Philippians 4:6

10. Even though Jesus was the Christ, and the Son of the living God, He found it necessary and important to spend time alone praying to His Father. Where did Jesus go to pray?

Mark 1:35

Mark 6:46

Luke 5:16

Luke 6:12

Luke 22:41

READ: John 17:1-26.
11. For whom did Jesus pray? Give references.

12. In John 17:20, 21, Jesus was concerned for His believers. What was this concern?

13. How often do you read your Bible and pray?

14. Is this often enough to keep you from withering spiritually? If not, what will you do to spend more time communicating with your heavenly Father?

15. How often do you spend time reading the Bible and praying with family members?

16. Are you satisfied with this arrangement? If not, what will you do to change the situation?

17. Why is it important for us to read the Bible and pray?

   Acts 17:11

   Ephesians 6:10-17

18. Can you think of any other reasons why it is important for us to read the Bible and pray? (Give a Bible reference if you know one.)

SPIRITUAL CHALLENGE: If you do not have a daily time of Bible reading and prayer, I want to encourage you to begin today. Find a slice of time during your busy day when you can be alone with the Lord. Talk to Him in prayer and read at least one chapter in the Bible daily. Make this a priority, or you will always be too busy.

If you already have a daily time of prayer and study, that's wonderful. Keep up the good work! Take time to improve where you feel weak. Best wishes to all of you as you draw closer to your Creator and Savior.

Chapter Three

Overdrawn

Bill and Nancy talked about money before their wedding. It didn't seem like such a big deal then, but now it was ruining their marriage.

Even though Nancy and Bill were both working full time, they still could not make ends meet. Every time finances were mentioned, it always developed into a heated argument.

Nancy was expecting their first child in seven short months, and financial problems interfered with the joy of her pregnancy. Bill and Nancy knew that the baby would add more expenses to their already stretched budget. Together they realized that they needed to do something. Bankruptcy would ruin their credit record, but it seemed like a quick solution that would clear their books and give them a fresh start.

Nancy pondered the idea of bankruptcy for several days. At first, Nancy thought she was doing her best with their budget, but she decided to make a list of possible ways she could cut back on spending. Nancy was hoping this would give her some new insight on the problem. She asked her husband to do the same. After their lists were completed, Bill and Nancy agreed to sit down and calmly discuss their dilemma together. They agreed not to blame each other, but to work together as a team.

Bill had dreams of buying a home. Nancy was determined to stay home and raise their children rather than sending them to day-care. Before discussing their problem, Bill and Nancy went to the Lord in prayer and asked Him to be their guide in this financial disaster. They set some goals and diligently went to work.

After spending the afternoon together, Bill and Nancy realized that most of Nancy's income went towards paying high interest on loans, overdrawn check penalties, and late charges. They discovered several ways to save money. This included shopping for bargains, buying sale items, and cutting coupons. Bill agreed to carpool to work, and Nancy saw the necessity of using leftover food instead of dumping it down the garbage disposal. They also agreed to take sack lunches to work instead of eating out every day, and all loose change was to be put into a special baby fund. They realized that it wasn't necessary to have the best of everything, and they decided to quit competing with their friends. Possessions in general had possessed them, creating a lot of unhappiness. Bill and Nancy laughed together as they cut all of their credit cards into confetti.

Seven months later, Bill and Nancy rejoiced at the birth of their first child, a little boy. The money in the baby fund provided the nursery with a beautiful used baby ensemble, and Nancy quit working two weeks before the baby was born. At last Bill and Nancy were debt free! Now they could begin saving for their new home.

Dear heavenly Father,

Please help me to always be a good steward of Your money. Help me to remember that You have promised me, through Your Word, that You will always provide for my needs. Help me to be aware of the fact that "needs" are different than "wants."

In Jesus' name, amen.

Memory verse: Proverbs 3:9

Honor the Lord with your wealth, with the firstfruits of all your crops.

1. List six mistakes Bill and Nancy made that contributed to their financial dilemma.

2. List at least eight things that this couple did to free themselves from this disaster.

3. How often does money become a problem in your home—always, sometimes, or never?

4. In what ways do finances interfere with relationships in your life?

5. Do you have many conflicts in your home based on financial burdens?

6. Bill and Nancy made several adjustments in order to save their marriage and correct their financial mistakes. Are your finances deterring you from developing a closer relationship with people you love? If so, what are you willing to sacrifice in order to obtain a stable relationship with other family members?

7. Sometimes financial problems can keep people from developing a relationship with the Lord as well. This was not the case with Bill and Nancy because they prayed to God for guidance and asked Him for help in solving their financial problems. Does your financial situation ever keep you from serving or obeying God?

8. Which is more important to you—God and eternal life, or your financial status? Give a reason for your answer.

READ: 1 Timothy 6:6-10.
9. What is great gain?

10. What will we take with us when we leave this world?

11. With what should we be content?

12. What happens to people who want to get rich?

13. What is "the root of all evil"?

14. What happens to many people who are eager for money?

15. What will you put aside in order to keep God first in your life?

16. Do you worry about money? If so, how often?

READ: Matthew 6:25-34.
17. About what does the Lord want us to be worried?

18. Does this mean that we should not work or try to balance our budgets? Why or why not?

READ: Ecclesiastes 5:10.

19. What does the writer consider meaningless?

READ: Philippians 4:19.

20. Do you believe this passage? Give a few reasons to support your answer.

21. When was the last time you planned a budget and set financial goals for your household?

SPIRITUAL CHALLENGE: Analyze your current financial situation. Write down your goals, desires, debts, and income. Then design a plan that will help you achieve your goals. If you are married, include your spouse, and work together at being good stewards of God's money. Be sure to include the Lord in your plans. Read Psalm 24:1, Proverbs 3:9, 1 Corinthians 16:2, and Hebrews 7:5 for spiritual guidance in planning your new budget.

Section Two
Heavy Duty

Dear reader,

When we "spring clean" our homes, it is important to clean all areas. This includes the nitty-gritty: cupboards, ovens, drawers, closets, and unseen corners that the average visitor never notices. This "heavy duty" cleaning is always difficult but nonetheless necessary to keep things in proper order.

Our bodies, or spiritual homes, which are temples of God, also need "spring cleaning" in order to remain pure and acceptable to the Lord. Quite often we have little or no trouble maintaining the "light and breezy," but there are many times when Christians try to put on the "finishing touches" without tending to any "heavy duty" cleaning first. This process can be risky, because sometimes we end up wearing a mask in efforts to hide the unattended cleaning within.

It is quite easy to deceive other people, but God knows the heart and all that it contains. He sees the hidden dirt when no one else can. That is why after much prayer, careful consideration, and counseling with several men and women in the church, I have decided to include some sensitive and very personal issues in this section of the book.

Reality is often ugly, and I realize that the nature of this material may be unpleasant for some of you to think about or discuss. But in order to clean out the accumulated dirt, you must dig into it wholeheartedly. My prayer for you is that you will commit to doing just that. If the church of Christ is going to be victorious, it is necessary for us to understand that ugly situations happen to Christians as well as to non-Christians. Oftentimes these crises leave emotional and spiritual wounds unless they are dealt with and resolved.

If you have escaped some of these trials, count your blessings. Hopefully these lessons will give you new insight in which you can help others who have not been so blessed. If you find yourself depicted in one of these stories, my prayer for you is that you will trust the Lord with all of your heart, that you too may be healed. The lives of real *people are portrayed in some of these stories, and I can assure you that with God, all things are possible—even complete healing where it hurts the most.*

As you continue your spiritual adventure in Spiritual Spring Cleaning, remember the encouragement of James 5:16: "Therefore confess your sins to each other and pray for each other so that you may be healed. The prayer of a righteous man is powerful and effective." My prayers go with you now and as you venture on.

In His precious love and service,

Debbie Schmid

Chapter Four

I'll Show Him

"Why can't he show some enthusiasm when he comes home from work?" Paula sulked. "I must not mean anything to him!"

Completely frustrated with her husband and their marriage, Paula no longer felt those warm feelings that filled her as a newlywed.

Night after night, her husband's arrival home from work was carbon-copied. His half-hearted smile and unenthusiastic "hello" left Paula feeling unloved and unimportant.

Every evening it was the same dull routine. Joe entered the house and immediately asked, "Is this the only mail that came?"

"Yes," Paula always answered.

Then Joe asked, "Did anyone call for me today?"

Paula's answers were the same night after night—either "No one called today," or "Your messages are next to the phone."

Without speaking another word, Joe disappeared into his home office until dinner was ready. Conversations during dinner were often brief and shallow.

"Oh, that man!" Paula complained. "What a bore!" She wondered whatever happened to "Hi, hon, how was your day?" or "Wow! It feels great to be home." Paula longed desperately for a warm hug or an intimate evening with Joe. They seldom kissed each other anymore, and Paula felt lonely and frustrated. Then her frustration changed to anger. Fury burned deep inside her.

"That's fine," she thought. "I think I'll pursue Ted's interest in me." Ted was a friend and coworker who had been interested in

Paula for quite some time. Paula's loneliness and desperate need for attention, missing in her marriage, were the deciding factors. "I'll show Joe that men still find me attractive. Maybe this will get his attention."

Several months later, Joe bubbled as he enthusiastically breezed through the kitchen. "Hi, hon, what's for dinner?"

"Pot roast," Paula replied.

"Oh, my favorite." With his arms wrapped around Paula's waist, Joe asked, "How soon?"

"Ten minutes," Paula answered.

"Do you mind if I go into my office to unwind until dinner is ready?"

"No, not at all."

Joe kissed Paula on the forehead, but before he left the room, he commented on the delicious smell of the meal cooking.

During dinner, conversation was warm from Joe's side of the table. Paula, on the other hand, was cool. Her answers were brief, and her words were chosen cautiously. Even her smile was reserved. "What's gotten into him?" she wondered.

Later that evening, Joe lovingly turned to Paula. "Honey, I've noticed your new attitude lately, and I appreciate it very much. I know I haven't always been the best husband, but things at the office have been in turmoil for quite some time. I'm sorry, Paula. Please forgive me."

Paula remained silent while Joe reached over to embrace her. "You're more beautiful than the day I married you," he whispered. "I love you. Thank you for being so patient and understanding."

Paula immediately withdrew from his side and harshly snapped, "How dare you!"

"What's wrong?" Joe innocently questioned. "Is it something I said?"

"I can't believe you!" she retorted. "For years I have been longing for your affection and warm conversation. Now that you're jealous, you turn on the charm and act innocent."

"Jealous? Innocent? Paula, what are you talking about?"

"Oh, play dumb . . . you know good and well that I've been having an affair with Ted."

"An affair! Paula, you can't be serious. Whatever tempted you into doing something so foolish?"

34

"You did!" she yelled.

"Me?" Joe asked in shock. "What did I do? For years I have worked myself ragged, trying my hardest to provide for you and our children, let alone all those crazy spending habits of yours, and this is the thanks I get. You have turned on me by defiling our wedding vows. I can't believe this."

Paula remained silent as Joe proceeded. "You go tell Ted that you don't want to see him again. Paula, are you listening to me?"

"Joe, I can't do that," Paula sobbed.

"Then I will!" Joe shouted as he picked up the telephone receiver. "I'll call him right now!"

"You can't, Joe," Paula insisted as she pulled the phone from his hand.

"Why not? You're mine, and I refuse to share you with another man."

"Joe, you don't understand. I'm pregnant, and Ted is the father of my baby."

Dear heavenly Father,

Please guide my thoughts and actions that I may not plan a trap for myself or depend on others to give me what only You can provide.

In Jesus' name, amen.

Memory verse: Romans 12:21
Do not be overcome by evil, but overcome evil with good.

By human nature, we all desire to feel loved and special. Sometimes those warm and happy feelings keep us strong during the darkest hours in our lives. But what happens to us when we don't receive what we want, need, or feel we deserve?

1. Explain how you react or respond to someone you feel is neglecting or disappointing you.

2. Are you satisfied with this behavior? If not, explain how you will change these actions.

READ: Romans 8:20, 21.
3. Why does God allow us to feel frustrated?

4. What do you feel Paula's main motives were for pursuing a relationship with Ted?

Paula expected Joe to meet her every need. When he didn't, she sought revenge against him for what she felt was unacceptable behavior on his part.

5. Read the following Scriptures, and write down what the Lord says about revenge.

Leviticus 19:18

Deuteronomy 32:35

Romans 12:17

Romans 12:19

Romans 12:21

1 Peter 3:9

6. What other problems can you detect in Paula's story?

7. List three possible solutions you feel would have been acceptable to God as opposed to the choice Paula made.

8. Like Paula, we all experience moments of emptiness and anxiety. How does anxiety generally affect you?

READ: Proverbs 12:25.
9. What does an anxious heart do to a person?

10. Can you think of a specific time when your heart felt anxious? How did those feelings of anxiety affect you? How did those anxious feelings affect the situation at the time?

READ: Philippians 4:6.
11. What are we supposed to be anxious about?

READ: 1 Peter 5:7.
12. What do the Scriptures tell us to do with our anxiety?

SPIRITUAL CHALLENGE: Write about another situation that made you anxious. Explain how you responded to that trial and describe the outcome. If you had the opportunity to experience a similar trial today, in what ways would you handle it differently?

Keep working on the areas in which you want to grow. If you are in the habit of feeling anxious over many situations, cast all your cares upon Him, and He will give you rest.

Chapter Five

Don't Blame Him

"I want a divorce," Paula demanded. "I can't remain in this marriage any longer."

"No, Paula, please don't go," Joe pleaded. "I love you, and I promise to love the baby as if it were our child. What can I do to convince you to stay?"

"Nothing," Paula answered.

"Honey, I forgive you," Joe continued. "Please, let's work through this together."

"No!" Paula snapped bitterly. "I have made up my mind, and I'm not changing it. You can have custody over our three children. I'll keep the baby. Ted wants to get married."

"Paula," Joe urged, "you are making a big mistake. Ted is an alcoholic and a violent man. I've known him for years. I'm afraid he will hurt you."

"He won't hurt me," Paula argued. "Ted is a warm and compassionate person. You're just jealous! Besides, this is what I have been looking for for years. Joe, I'm not changing my mind."

"Paula, I love you. Please . . ." Joe insisted.

"I don't care if you love me. I haven't loved you in many years. I have absolutely no desire to work things out between us. As far as I'm concerned, this subject is closed."

Paula stormed out of the house, slamming the door behind her. Joe tearfully watched her from the picture window as she drove off into the evening sunset.

Five years later...

Paula sat empty-handed and homeless. Her clothing was torn, her face bruised, and her baby girl, now four years old, had been taken from her and placed in a foster home. While sobbing uncontrollably, she muttered repeatedly, "I hate Joe! He ruined my life. I can never forgive that man. Look what he has done to me," she told the social worker.

The social worker patiently listened and then spoke. "Paula, let's talk about Joe. It sounds like you need to discuss some things that are upsetting you."

Paula made it quite clear that her current dilemma was Joe's fault. After listening for about thirty minutes, the social worker looked Paula in the eyes and softly said, "Paula, I'm going to give you an assignment. Before we proceed tomorrow, I would like you to consider these questions. First, who chose to be unfaithful and leave your first marriage and three children behind? Second, who loved you and begged you to stay? And third, who bruised you and hurt you this morning? Please, be honest with yourself. Here's some more tissue. You can stay in the temporary housing unit until we work through some of these painful issues."

"Thank you," Paula said.

The social worker gave Paula a hug and escorted her to a room where she could rest. "Here is a fresh outfit for you to wear. I'll see you tomorrow morning. Good night."

Dear heavenly Father,

Please help me to face my own mistakes and their consequences and not to blame others for my problems. Help me to remember that Your love is forgiving, and with it perfect love can be accomplished.

In Jesus' name I pray, amen.

Memory verse: James 4:17

Anyone, then, who knows the good he ought to do and doesn''t do it, sins.

1. Give several reasons why you feel Paula decided to leave Joe, even after he forgave her and released her from the terrible mistake she made.

2. What was Paula looking for in a relationship?

3. In your opinion, what were Paula's three biggest mistakes?

4. After reality struck and Paula's life crumbled down around her, why did she continue to blame Joe for her unhappiness?

5. How do you normally deal with crises that make you unhappy?

6. Can you think of a situation in your own life where you rushed ahead of God's timing and tried to "fix" or "change" a situation yourself? Explain.

7. What were the results?

8. If the results were bad or less than what you expected, did you take responsibility for the outcome or did you shift the blame onto another person, perhaps even God?

9. If you blamed another person, what kind of relationship do you share with that person today?

10. Read the following verses. Next to each one, write down what can keep us from trouble.

Proverbs 28:14

James 5:16

11. Read Proverbs 17:15. What kinds of things does the Lord detest?

12. What advice does the Bible give us concerning our anger?

Psalm 37:8

Proverbs 14:17

Proverbs 16:32

Ecclesiastes 7:9

James 1:19, 20

13. When we trust in something other than God to meet our needs, the Bible refers to that as idolatry. What do the Scriptures teach about idols?

1 John 5:21

Exodus 20:3, 4

14. Do you think it is possible for a person to be an "idol" to us as well as an "object"? Explain your answer.

15. What excellent piece of advice does the Lord give us in Matthew 7:1-5?

Facing our faults can be a difficult and humbling experience. Many times people find it easier to shift the blame onto another person rather than taking responsibility for their own behavior. Unfortunately, this does not bring resolution into our lives. On the contrary, it often results in further complications. It is important for each of us to honestly examine ourselves and take responsibility for our own actions. It is through the taking of responsibility for ourselves that we come to grips with our own feelings and learn to rely on the only One who can provide us with the abundant life we all desperately desire. That One is none other than Christ Jesus Himself.

SPIRITUAL CHALLENGE: If you are guilty of judging or blaming other people for your trials or unhappiness, take heart. Ask the Lord to help you deal with your own behavior and its consequences. Then seek to release yourself and/or other people from your bondage. Remember, you are not alone if you belong to Christ. With His help, you can do it!

The first series about Joe and Paula turned out rather hopelessly. Paula's fury burned, sin entered, the fire was fed, and in no time at all their marriage was in ruins. It is unfortunate that these things really happen in our society, but the outcome does not have to be so bleak.

Before starting today's lesson, please reread the story in chapter four entitled "I'll Show Him." Then, let's take a look at how this same situation, if handled differently, could have turned out.

Chapter Six

Cleaning Up the Rubbish

Shocked, Joe glared at Paula in disbelief. "You've been having an affair and now you're pregnant with another man's baby? I can't believe what I'm hearing! Paula, why didn't you tell me you were unhappy in our marriage? I had no idea...."

Paula was quick to interrupt. "You had no idea because you are never here! That business has become top priority in your life! The children and I never see you anymore. Day after day you miss out on all the happenings around here. When was the last time you spent some quality time with any of us?"

"I realize I have been gone a lot lately," Joe admitted, "and I'm sorry. But that doesn't give you permission to have an affair! Don't you understand, Paula? I love you. The reason I work so hard is to provide you and the children with the best of everything. You don't even appreciate all I do for you, and...."

Once again Paula interrupted. "We don't need the best of everything! We need you here spending time with us, not your stupid computers!" Paula's voice started to change from an angry yell to a tender cry. "Joe, I miss you when you're always gone. How can I help you understand that I've been lonely for a very long time? I feel like I'm just your maid, cook, and babysitter."

Joe's voice also became calmer when he realized more truths behind Paula's motives for being unfaithful to him. "Honey, you know that is not how I feel about you," he said tenderly as he handed her some tissue and held her close to his side.

"Joe, do you realize that this is the first time in over a year that you have held me close and shown any concern whatsoever? I can't believe we're actually discussing our feelings. I didn't think this was possible anymore."

"Paula, why didn't you come to me before all of these issues erupted?"

"I don't know," Paula replied. "I just assumed you didn't care anymore. I'm sorry."

"I guess we both have been unfaithful to one another in a way," Joe concluded. "I haven't given our marriage what it has needed for a long time. Now that I think about it, I've been married to my business. What are we going to do now?"

"I don't know," Paula admitted. "When I decided to pursue a relationship with Ted, I was so furious with you and your lack of attentiveness to me and the children. I never expected it to develop into a mess like this. I was only trying to get your attention."

"Well, you have accomplished that!" Joe said. "But where do we go from here?"

"I have no idea."

"Do you love Ted?"

"I don't know. I'm so confused, Joe."

"Paula, I must be honest with you. I am very hurt and upset. I'm asking you to please stop seeing Ted immediately so we can restore our marriage."

"What about the baby?" Paula asked.

"You're not thinking of aborting it, are you?" questioned Joe.

"Well, no," Paula answered, confused. "But I can't stay here and have this baby."

"Why not?" Joe asked.

"Because . . . well, it wouldn't be right."

"Neither is divorce."

"Joe, you can't be serious. Are you telling me that you want to mend our marriage despite what I have done to you?"

"Why not? I still love you. I married you for better or for worse. Apparently this is part of the 'worse.' Paula, we've been through so much already in this marriage. You're not thinking of just throwing away our fifteen-year relationship, are you?"

"I honestly didn't think I would have to make this decision, Joe. I expected the worst. This all comes as a complete shock to me."

"I think it would be best if we got some rest tonight. It's nearly three in the morning. I'm not going to work tomorrow. We need to finish this discussion and make some important decisions. Things will work out for the best, you'll see."

Neither Joe nor Paula slept well that night. The next day, they spent several hours alone discussing their deepest needs and feelings. Paula agreed to stop seeing Ted, and Joe promised to be more attentive to his family. After they reached these conclusions, they went to the Lord in prayer and gave the situation to Him.

Dear heavenly Father,

Please help me to remain faithful to my husband all the days of our lives. Please give us both the patience and communication skills necessary to have a strong and open relationship—not full of evil plans that will harm ourselves or our loved ones, but words that will build and strengthen the relationship we share with you and with each other.

In Jesus' name I pray, amen.

Memory verse: Proverbs 15:1
A gentle answer turns away wrath, but a harsh word stirs up anger.

In the story "I'll Show Him," we discovered several problems between Joe and Paula. Let's quickly review the main points.

A. Lack of communication.

B. Lack of intimacy.

C. Lack of commitment.

D. Paula depended on Joe to meet all her needs, and when he didn't live up to her expectations, she took revenge.

E. Joe spent too much time at work and not enough time with his family.

1. List at least five important interactions that were happening between Joe and Paula in this story that were different than in "I'll Show Him."

2. What does "communication" mean to you?

3. List several different ways in which communication is shared between two people.

4. What helpful tips do the Scriptures provide for us, especially when we are struggling?

John 14:1

John 16:33

2 Corinthians 2:7

1 Thessalonians 5:14

READ: Ephesians 4:26, 27.
5. When should we resolve our anger and why?

6. Many times when we are angry, disappointed, or hurting, we have a human tendency to say or do things that we later regret. Explain what Ephesians 4:29-32 means to you.

READ: James chapter 3.
7. The majority of our communication is done verbally. List the many things a tongue is capable of doing, although it is small in size. Give the verse reference with each answer.

8. What should a Christian do with his or her tongue?

James 1:26

Proverbs 21:23

9. Read the following verses and fill in the blank beside each reference. The Lord detests:

Psalm 34:13 _____

Proverbs 6:16-19 _____

Proverbs 17:20 _____

Proverbs 26:28 _____

10. According to the following verses, what should we do with our tongues?

Proverbs 21:23

Proverbs 25:11

Proverbs 25:15

11. According to the following Scriptures, what simple principles should we try to remember when we speak to others?

Proverbs 15:1

Proverbs 25:23

2 Timothy 2:24

James 1:19, 20

SPIRITUAL CHALLENGE: How do you speak to others? Do you season your speech with love (Colossians 4:6), or do you use it as a weapon to hurt others?

This week, concentrate on your speech and communication with others. If a person has recently wronged you and you feel angry towards him or her, try to comunicate with that person in a way that would please the Lord.

Be careful of your tone of voice. Sometimes it is not *what* we say that is so hurtful, but it is *how* we say it.

Chapter Seven

Despite Our Weaknesses

Seven months later, Joe came up behind Paula and wrapped his loving arms around her pregnant tummy. "I love you," he whispered. "Have you felt any more contractions?"

"No," Paula replied. "I think it was a false alarm."

"I can't wait for the baby to be born," he said softly, kissing her on the neck. "I wonder if it's a boy or a girl."

"It's not fair!" Paula tearfully said.

"What's not fair?" Joe asked.

"Joe, for the past eight months I have struggled with this pregnancy. I don't understand how you can love me after what I have done to you. I'm such an awful person."

Joe warmly hugged her. "Honey, I've told you over and over again that I have forgiven you. Remember the discussion we had when this first happened?"

Paula nodded.

"Marriage is a partnership. Part of the reason all of this happened was because I wasn't here for you."

"That shouldn't have mattered. This isn't supposed to happen to Christians. I should have turned to God for comfort, not Ted. I was so bitter and angry with you. Now I regret what I have done."

"So, you made a mistake. We all do. The important thing is that we learn from them and turn away from our sins. You have done that, Paula. Don't be so hard on yourself. Forgive yourself and let go. What's done is done."

"I can't," sobbed Paula. "I don't deserve to be forgiven."

"None of us do," Joe replied. "But that's why Jesus came. Despite all of our weaknesses and foolishness, He still loves us. We need to do our part and let Him do His."

"It's so hard for me to accept that truth, Joe."

"I know," Joe continued, "but if we don't accept His unconditional love and forgiveness, then Jesus died for nothing. And the reason I still love you is because Jesus still loves me. We need to love each other the way He loves us."

Paula slowly walked away, crying. "I need to be alone with God."

Three weeks later, Paula gave birth to a precious little girl. Joe and Paula named her Faith Ann Joy (and called her Joy) because their faithfulness in God and in their marriage had been restored, and their marriage had turned to joy as a result of her life.

In time, Paula was able to forgive herself and trusted fully in the Lord to meet her needs. Her faith blossomed like a beautiful rose, and Joe and Paula remained happily married following their crisis.

Dear heavenly Father,

Help me to understand Your unconditional love and to accept it. And despite my weaknesses, please help me learn to love others in the same way, unconditionally and without reservation.

In Jesus' name I pray, amen.

Memory Verse: Isaiah 53:6

We all, like sheep, have gone astray, each of us has turned to his own way; and the Lord has laid on him the iniquity of us all.

1. Give some reasons why you think Joe was so willing to forgive Paula of her marital unfaithfulness.

2. Why was it so difficult for Paula to forgive herself?

3. Define "unconditional love."

4. What do you feel is necessary in order to love someone unconditionally?

5. Do you find it difficult to love others unconditionally?

6. Have you ever been in a hurtful situation that challenged you to love someone unconditionally? If so, how did that situation turn out?

READ: Matthew 7:1-5.

7. Unconditional love requires a tremendous amount of love, commitment, patience, and understanding on the giver's part. What important principles should we remember when we find another person at fault?

8. In what way did Joe apply this principle in his unfortunate situation with Paula?

READ: 1 Corinthians 13:1-13.

9. In verses 1-3, list the illustrations used to describe a person without love.

10. What is love according to verses 4-8a?

11. List at least six ways in which these principles of love were applied in Joe and Paula's situation.

12. Choose six virtues of love and describe how you apply these principles in your own life when loving others around you.

13. Now read verse 13. Which quality holds the greatest value of the three? Why?

14. According to the Scriptures, everyone needs God's unconditional love. Romans 3:23 says, "for all have sinned and fall short of the glory of God." Since we are all in need of a Savior, God sent His only begotten Son to earth to be our perfect sacrifice. Read the following verses. Beside each one, write how God's unconditional love spilled over to your benefit.

Isaiah 53:5

Isaiah 53:6

Isaiah 53:11

Isaiah 53:12

Romans 5:8

15. How is God's love described in Jeremiah 31:3?

16. How can we know that Jesus loves us (1 John 3:16)?

17. From where does love come?

18. Why should we love one another (1 John 4:11)?

19. How is God described in 1 John 4:8?

READ: John 3:16 and 1 John 4:9, 10.
20. How did God show His love among us?

READ: Ephesians 2:4-7.
21. Why did God make us alive in Christ despite the fact that we were dead in our sins?

22. Crucifixion was an extremely cruel, slow, agonizing, and tortuous death penalty. Jesus had the power to refuse to face the cross. yet because of His love and obedience to His Father in heaven, He obeyed, suffered, and died for you and me. Even while hanging on the cross, Jesus never once became hateful. Instead He demonstrated His unconditional love for others until "it was finished." Below are some verses which refer to His last words spoken from the cross. Beside each one, write how He continued to love unconditionally despite the awful circumstances He was experiencing.

Luke 23:32-37

Luke 23:38-43

John 19:25-27

23. When did Jesus finally give up His spirit (John 19:28-30)?

SPIRITUAL CHALLENGE: Perhaps there is someone in your life right now who is in need of your unconditional love. Think of ways in which you can apply the principles of love from 1 Corinthians chapter 13. Jesus paid a tremendous price to teach us unconditional love. Let's not allow His suffering to be in vain. Instead, may we all trust in His power to help us demonstrate His unconditional love to others in all situations.

Chapter Eight

Defiled

"Stop it! You're hurting me!" Megan mumbled as her betrayer pressed his muscular hands firmly over her mouth.

"Shut up!" he demanded. "And remember—if you tell anyone about this, I will kill you. Got it?"

Megan turned "sweet sixteen" just a few days before her uncle Roger arrived from out of state. He was staying with Megan's family for the summer to help work on the farm, but the joy of his arrival had turned into a painful and endless nightmare for Megan. Each night, after everyone was asleep, Roger crept into Megan's bedroom to sexually assault her.

The entire family loved Uncle Roger. They saw him as a dashing young man full of fun and vigor. But Megan hated him! Her most valuable possession, her virginity, had been confiscated and defiled. She felt dirty and angry. Megan wanted to confide in her parents. They had always been so close, but with a death threat from Uncle Roger she felt unable to take the risk.

Ten years passed, and Megan continued to harbor this horrible secret. She constantly hoped and prayed that her anger would cease, but a bitter root had sprouted, and it began to choke out her beautiful, fun-loving spirit. Uncle Roger's visit ten summers ago still haunted Megan. And now it was ruining her marriage. Megan found it difficult to be intimate with her husband, and as the years passed she became more and more depressed. Sometimes she felt so much pain that she wanted to die.

That autumn, Megan received an invitation to her cousin Jody's wedding. The moment she read it, Megan became furious and burst out in a sudden explosion of anger. "How dare she!" Megan shouted. "How could Jody invite me to her wedding after what her father did to me? I hate Uncle Roger! I wish he were dead," she sobbed.

The following weeks challenged Megan with many discontented feelings. The more she thought about her outrage, the more she realized that, regardless of what Uncle Roger did to her many years ago, she needed to attend Jody's wedding. After all, Jody had always been her favorite cousin.

Megan and her husband cautiously entered the church building. Immediately Megan's eyes scanned the auditorium, looking for Uncle Roger. Her hands were clammy and her face flushed with fear as the bridal procession began. Megan's insides suddenly froze as Jody came into view. She hadn't seen Uncle Roger since that summer of horror ten years earlier.

Panic struck! Megan jabbed her husband with her elbow and whispered, "Where is Uncle Roger? Why is Aunt Polly walking Jody down the aisle alone?"

Her husband shrugged his shoulders questioningly and answered, "I don't know. This is all a shock to me, too."

During the reception, Megan learned that her uncle was in prison for several counts of rape and murder. Megan's icy heart melted, and when she arrived home she sat down and wrote to Uncle Roger.

After several months of communicating regularly by mail, Megan was able to forgive her uncle. As the result of her efforts by mail and the teaching of a Christian fellow prisoner, Uncle Roger repented of his sins and was baptized into Christ. The morning following his execution, Megan wept tears of joy mixed with sorrow. "If only I had told my parents," she thought, "perhaps Uncle Roger and his victims would still be alive today, and so many other young girls would not have been defiled."

Dear heavenly Father,

What a blessing it is to know that no sin is too great for Your love and forgiveness. Help me to always humble myself, that I may draw others to You regardless of the pain they have caused me. Please keep Your warmth close to my heart that it may never become hard and frozen.

In Jesus' name, amen.

Memory Verse: Hebrews 12:15
See to it that no one misses the grace of God and that no bitter root grows up to cause trouble and defile many.

1. What did Uncle Roger do to Megan that planted the seed for destruction in her life?

2. Why didn't Megan confide in her parents?

3. Why do you think Megan became more bitter and angry toward her uncle as the years passed?

4. What combination of reasons do you think caused Megan to have a change in heart towards Uncle Roger?

5. What does it mean to be "defiled"?

6. Has anyone ever "defiled" you or caused you unjustified pain? If so, what happened?

7. Describe the pain you felt as a result of this unfortunate experience.

8. How has this situation affected you, perhaps even today?

9. How do you feel about this person today?

10. According to your answers to the previous questions, do you consider this situation to be resolved or unresolved?

11. Are you at peace with this situation? If not, have you forgiven this person?

12. Examining your own life, have you ever "betrayed" or "defiled" another person? If so, who was that person and what happened?

13. What is your relationship with that person today?

14. Are you at peace with that situation? If not, what can you do to change that?

15. Do either of the previously mentioned situations require you to forgive yourself? If so, have you truly forgiven yourself and released yourself from the bondage and pain of past hurts and failures?

As human beings, sometimes it is very difficult for us to forgive someone who has hurt us deeply. Even tougher than forgiving others is forgiving ourselves of past sins and failures. Many times it takes a great deal of strength and courage to face those deep wounds and resolve them.

The two basic root issues involved in healing from any painful situation are *identification* and *forgiveness*. Once we identify the problem and understand where our pain is coming from, we can better determine what actions are necessary to forgive and let go of the pain.

Sometimes it is helpful to remember that the Lord requires us to forgive others. Jesus very unselfishly gave His life in order that we could receive forgiveness of our sins and eternal life.

Let's carefully consider the following Scripture verses and questions and try to obtain personal application for our own lives.

16. How does the Lord want us to act toward others who have sinned against us?

Matthew 6:14, 15

Mark 11:25

Ephesians 4:32

Colossians 3:13

17. How many times does the Lord tell us to forgive others?

Matthew 18:21, 22

Luke 17:4

Forgiveness means to fully pardon another person's transgressions against you; to cease to feel bitterness or anger towards the transgressor; to let go of the pain and to love that person unconditionally regardless of the violation; to set that person free from bondage, thus setting yourself free.

18. According to the Bible, who has sinned?

Isaiah 53:6

Romans 3:23

READ: Acts 13:38 and Ephesians 1:7.
19. From whom do we receive forgiveness of sins?

20. According to Psalm 103:3, what does God promise us? Do you think this refers to physical or spiritual diseases and why? Give other references if possible.

Because of God's tremendous love for us, He has provided eternal hope and salvation through Jesus Christ our Lord. It is obvious that in order to believe in God, we must *hear* the gospel message. Once we *believe*, the Lord wants us to *repent*, or turn away from our sinful ways, and *confess* Jesus as Lord. We then are instructed to crucify our old selves by being buried with Christ in the watery grave of *baptism*. This simple act of obedience, with a sincere and believing heart toward Christ, puts us in contact with the blood of Christ. The Lord purifies us and gives us His promised gift of the Holy Spirit to help us live godly lives in an ungodly world.

21. Have you been biblically forgiven and added to the kingdom of God? Remember, God forgives. Have you let Him?

SPIRITUAL CHALLENGE: *If you are not a Christian*, and have not received God's forgiveness for your sins or the promised gift of the Holy Spirit, please consider this for your own life. The appendix of this book has lesson material entitled "The Lord's Perfect Plan for Salvation." It has been included to aid you in your quest for eternal salvation. Through prayer, ask the Lord for wisdom and guidance as you study His will for your life.

If you are a Christian, but have unresolved hurts, bitterness, or anger toward another person, seek the Lord for guidance and wisdom concerning this trial. Ask Him to provide the strength you need to resolve this conflict. It might be necessary to talk to the person who has hurt you, write a letter, give them a call, or pursue other appropriate actions. Once you allow that burden to be lifted from your heart, you will truly begin to experience the new and abundant life in Christ Jesus.

A NOTE OF CHEER...

Jesus was willing to hang on a cross and die for you and me that we might be forgiven. He provides us with the strength, courage, and selfless example necessary to forgive others. Won't you do that for Him, today?

Chapter Nine

Identical Strangers

Judy heard her sister's voice coming over the telephone. "Hi, sis. It's me, Diane. I'm planning a business trip out east, and I have an unusually long layover between flights. I was wondering if you would like to meet me for lunch?" Judy eagerly accepted her sister's invitation. They hadn't seen each other in years.

Three days later, as Judy drove to the airport cafe, she was overwhelmed with feelings of insecurity and nervousness. "What can Diane and I possibly talk about for three hours?" she wondered. They had been complete opposites while growing up, and in later years distance had kept them apart.

Judy's mind drifted back to her childhood years. She clearly remembered how Diane did everything just right! Diane was the one who was naturally pretty, tidy, pleasant, and successful. She appeared to be self-confident, and she had the determination to meet her goals. Her marriage seemed perfect, and her children were pure joy.

Judy, however, had been the wallflower—the daughter with poor grades, a messy room, no dates, and no desire to compete with Diane. Even as an adult, Judy felt like a failure. Her relationship with her husband was strained, and her three children were wild and disobedient.

As Judy approached the airport parking lot, she noticed Diane patiently waiting for her never-on-time sister. Judy also noticed that Diane was even more beautiful than she remembered. She parked the car, sighed deeply, and peeled her sweaty hands off the steering wheel. Her legs were weak, and her feet were heavy as lead. With much effort, she lifted herself out of the car, locked the door, and slowly walked toward Diane.

Upon meeting, they embraced and tears filled their eyes. Judy suddenly realized how much she had missed Diane over the past several years. They had so much catching up to do, and only three short hours!

During lunch, tears began to flow from Diane's eyes. For over an hour she told Judy that many of her dreams had failed and that she felt unattractive and disillusioned with life. Diane felt she was unorganized and unsuccessful. Judy was shocked. "This can't be," she thought. "Surely not Diane! We must be talking about me."

As their conversation unfolded, Diane and Judy realized that they were "identical strangers." They both were struggling with life's disappointments and searching for inner peace, yet Diane had managed to fool many people, including her sister, for years.

That night Judy lay awake in bed and thought, "Does the Lord really want me to feel so poorly about myself and the life He has given me to live? There must be more to life than trials and disappointment." At 2:00 A.M., she got up and began to search the Scriptures. She knew that the Lord would have answers to her dilemma.

Dear heavenly Father,

Help me to discover myself and the potential within. Please comfort and lead me as I search for inner peace, and help me to see the beauty within myself that You have carefully created and selected for me. Then help me to let that inner peace spill over into my relationships with my husband and family and all with whom I come into contact.

In Jesus' name I pray, amen.

Memory Verse: Psalm 139:13, 14

For you created my inmost being; you knit me together in my mother's womb. I praise you because I am fearfully and wonderfully made; your works are wonderful, I know that full well.

1. How do you rate yourself? (L=low, A=average, H=high)

_____ physically attractive   _____ spiritually sound
_____ patient   _____ at peace within
_____ polite   _____ selfish
_____ caring   _____ rude
_____ successful   _____ hostile
_____ demanding   _____ kind

2. Are you happy with who you are?

3. If you could change something about your outer appearance, what would that be?

4. Is this a reachable goal? If so, what will you do to reach that goal?

5. What would you like to change about your inner self?

6. Have you ever heard others talk about you? If so, what kinds of things were said? List both positive and negative remarks.

7. Were all of these comments true?

8. How did the positive comments make you feel?

9. How did the negative comments affect you?

10. Do you believe everything you hear? If so, why?

11. How much do you value your life?

12. Are you a person who tends to bury yourself in self-pity, or do you tend to reach out to others regardless of the circumstances around you?

13. How often do you depend on others to meet these needs?

	ALWAYS	SOMETIMES	NEVER
Love	_____	_____	_____
Assurance	_____	_____	_____
Acceptance	_____	_____	_____
Security	_____	_____	_____

14. On whom do you depend to meet these needs (more than anyone else)?

15. Does this person ever let you down?

16. How do you react to this disappointment?

17. Read the following Bible verses. Next to each verse, write which need (love, assurance, acceptance, or security) the Lord will meet for us and why.

Romans 8:15-17

Colossians 1:21, 22

Titus 1:2

1 John 3:16

With God, our needs will be met.

READ: Psalm 139:13-16.

18. What do these verses mean to you?

19. How do these verses make you feel? Explain your answer.

20. How do we know that we are special to God and that He really loves us?

1 Peter 5:7

1 John 3:16

21. As Christians, we can draw near to God, our Creator and heavenly Father. What promises do these Scripture verses give us?

Romans 8:12-17

2 Corinthians 5:17

Colossians 1:21, 22

SPIRITUAL CHALLENGE: If you are not satisfied with yourself, give this burden to God. We are made in His image, and He wants us to be at peace with what He has created. Work on the areas that you are unhappy with, and seek God for fulfillment of your needs met. Other people often let us down or bring disappointments into our lives, but the Lord will never leave or forsake us (Hebrews 13:5). Personal satisfaction can sometimes be difficult to achieve, but with Christ all things are possible.

Chapter Ten

Genuine Beauty

For several months following Heather's conversion to Christ, she found herself consumed with insecurities. Coming out of the world, she needed to learn about living the Christian life from the bottom rung up.

Although Heather was sincere about her new faith and commitment, the truth of the matter was simple: Heather was very ignorant when it came to biblical and spiritual knowledge.

On Sunday mornings, she tried to listen carefully to the preacher's message, but quite often Heather found her attention turning elsewhere.

The greatest lessons that Heather learned were the ones she saw. Yes, Heather was indeed a people watcher! During the worship service, Heather carefully observed other Christian women and took special note of their righteousness.

Heather noticed their attitudes toward their husbands and children. She recognized the fact that many of the women wore inexpensive clothing and simple hairstyles. Several women wore very little jewelry or makeup, if any, and none of them came across as stuffy or proud. Rather, they were surrounded by a radiance of peace and beauty that enticed Heather.

Heather kept wondering, "What is it that makes these women so attractive? Even after a day at the beauty shop and a new outfit, I never look that beautiful." She was eager to learn their secret.

As time passed and Heather's faith increased, she realized that genuine beauty is not something that comes from the outside, but instead comes from within. Genuine beauty is the kind of beauty that only God can provide through the working of His Holy Spirit.

Dear heavenly Father,

Regardless of my life before the cross, please help me to become beautiful within, for it is inner beauty that radiates Your love and makes me genuinely beautiful, both inside and out.

In Jesus' name I pray, amen.

Memory Verse: Proverbs 31:30

Charm is deceptive, and beauty is fleeting; but a woman who fears the Lord is to be praised.

1. Define "beauty."

2. List ten qualities attributed to "outer beauty"—what do others notice? (Example: cleanliness)

READ: Galatians 5:22-25.

3. List ten positive qualities (fruit of the Spirit) attributed to "inner beauty" in column A. In column B, write the antonym (opposite) of each positive quality listen in column A.

Column A
(example: love)

Column B
(example: hate)

4. "As water reflects a face, so a man's heart reflects the man" (Proverbs 27:19). What does this verse mean to you? Does this verse motivate you to change something in your life? If so, start working toward that goal today.

5. Review questions two and three. Do you put more emphasis on your inner beauty or on your outer beauty? Explain.

READ: 1 Peter 3:1-6 and 1 Timothy 2:9-15.
6. Describe at least eight different ways that holy women of the past, who put their trust in God, made themselves beautiful.

7. Do you think those verses apply to women today? Why or why not?

8. Reread this week's memory verse, Proverbs 31:30. What is more important than beauty?

9. Consider inner and outer beauty. Of the two, which area do you feel you need to work on in your own life?

10. Has anyone ever complimented you on your character? If so, what did they say?

11. Are you being the very best example of Christ that you can be? If not, what will you do to change that?

SPIRITUAL CHALLENGE: Our actions, behavior, and appearance are the only sermons some people will ever hear. Below are two sections, one for inner beauty and one for outer beauty. Write down specific goals on how you want to mature in these areas. Then seek the Lord for His counsel. He will help you become genuinely beautiful from the inside out.

Inner beauty   Outer beauty

Section Three

Finishing Touches

Chapter Eleven

That's Not Fair

As Nicole's Christian walk progressed and time elapsed, she was horrified to learn that Christians suffer. Day after day, trials continued to consume not only her life, but also the lives of those around her.

"Oh, Anne, you can't be serious. The doctor says that George has Alzheimer's disease? I'm so sorry to hear that—and right when you both were planning to enjoy your retirement."

"Becky, I had no idea your teenage son was addicted to drugs and alcohol. Is there anything I can do to help? He was always such a good little boy."

"Tyler has leukemia. I can't believe it! He's only seven years old. Isn't there anything else the doctors can do for him?"

"We'll pray for you, Andy. Losing your family business must be awful. Do you have any ideas for your future?"

"I'm sorry, children. Mommy won't be coming home anymore. A drunk driver slammed into her car while she was driving home from the grocery store. She passed away just a few moments ago."

"I regret to tell you the bad news, Mrs. Jones, but your newborn baby has Down's syndrome."

"Why, Lord, why?" Nicole kept asking. "Why are You allowing Your children to suffer like this? Don't You love us enough to keep us free from suffering and pain? That's not fair!" she concluded time after time. "It's just not fair!"

Nicole had no idea what had made her believe that Christianity would be a trial-free, painless life. It was difficult for her to grasp the real fact that Christians do suffer and that God's ways are, obviously, much different than her own.

As Nicole grew in her faith and knowledge of Christ, she learned many important facts about Jesus. She was deeply touched to learn about the sufferings of her Lord, not only on the cross, but many times throughout His life. She meditated on the fact that Jesus, the Savior of the world, was tempted and tried just as Christians are today, and yet He endured without sin.

Nicole realized that the innocent Son of God was hungry, tired, tempted, beaten, mocked, spit upon, and nailed on the cross. Why, Lord, why? So that all of our transgressions could be forgiven. And those who choose to follow Him will inherit His gift of eternal life. As Nicole pondered these many truths she concluded, "That's not fair! But I'm so thankful for His abundant love."

Dear heavenly Father,

Thank You for not treating me as my sins deserve and for sending Jesus who was so willing to suffer and die, even though it wasn't fair. Help me to always remember that You understand my pain and that You will provide the strength and courage I need to endure each trial in my life.

In Jesus' name I pray, amen.

Memory verse: Psalm 46:1
God is our refuge and strength, an ever-present help in trouble.

1. What unreal expectations did Nicole have after becoming a Christian?

2. When Christians suffered, what did Nicole think?

3. What important truth did Nicole understand after she became more grounded in the faith?

4. What was Nicole's final conclusion?

5. How do you react to those "unfair" kinds of trials?

6. When we face trials of many kinds, what should we do according to the following Scriptures?

Psalm 42:11

Psalm 55:22

Psalm 62:8

7. Who provides the righteous man with strength or deliverance in times of trouble?

Psalm 34:19

Psalm 46:1

Psalm 121:2

READ: Hebrews 12:7-11.
8. How should the Christian view hardships?

9. Why does God discipline us?

Reread Hebrews 12:11, 12.
10. What does proper discipline produce?

11. Why should all Christians desire discipline from God?

READ: James 1:2-4, 12.
12. What develops perseverance?

13. Why is perseverance so important?

READ: James 1:13, 14.
14. What are the main differences between discipline and temptation?

15. What promise does God give us concerning temptation in 1 Corinthians 10:13?

READ: 1 Peter 1:6, 7.
16. Why should we rejoice when we face many trials?

17. According to 2 Corinthians 1:3, 4, we share two things with Christ. What are they? (What is God to us?)

18. What excellent advice do we receive from Proverbs 3:5?

19. What other beautiful and comforting promise does God give us in Hebrews 13:5?

20. Read the following verses. Beside each one, write its spiritual application. Then apply the messages to yourself to make it more personal.

Isaiah 29:16

Isaiah 64:8

Jeremiah 18:6

Romans 9:21

21. Do you think it was fair for Jesus to be crucified for our sins?

22. Have you ever thanked Him for what He has done for you?

SPIRITUAL CHALLENGE: If you have never thanked the Lord for what He has done for you, think more about the great sacrifice that was made and let the Lord know how you feel about His unselfish love and obedience.

The next time life challenges you with a "that's not fair" trial, put the biblical principles that we learned in this lesson into practice and lean on Him one hundred percent. Remember, His ways are not ours, and God truly does know what is best.

Chapter Twelve

God's Healing

Brooke rolled over in bed and squinted her eyes to read the time on the clock. It was only 2:00 A.M, July 19. Several hours of restlessness had passed, and still Brooke could not sleep.

Another half hour passed. Brooke decided to put on her robe and go out to the living room. As she slowly paced the room, she relived the past once again. "Why, Lord, why?" she wondered. "It's been several years now, and I still don't understand why my ex-fiancé broke our engagement only weeks before the wedding."

Since that time, Brooke had met, fallen in love with, and married a wonderful man. However, the wound to her pride and self-esteem left by her ex-fiancé's actions remained and her agonizing questions were still unanswered. "Lord," she prayed through her tears, "please help me understand my pain. Help me resolve this issue once and for all. I cannot bear this any longer."

After praying, Brooke wrote a letter to her ex-fiancé, forgiving him of the pain his decision had brought to her. She never expected to give it to him. She simply wrote it in search of healing. At 5:00 A.M., Brooke returned to bed and immediately fell asleep.

Every day, without ceasing, Brooke prayed faithfully concerning this open wound. She knew in her heart that God would provide the ointment necessary for complete healing—she just didn't know when it would take place.

One evening in September, the telephone rang. "Hello," the caller said. "Do you know who this is?"

Brooke paused. It was her ex-fiancé. "Yes," she nervously answered. "Why are you calling?"

"I bumped into your brother when I was home on vacation. We talked about you, and I asked him for your phone number. I would like to come visit you. Would that be okay?" he asked.

"I'll have to discuss this with my husband," she replied in shock. "I'll call you back later."

Brooke knew that the Lord was at work in this situation. She had never asked Him to bring her ex-fiancé back into her life, but she had prayed for healing. Her ex-fiancé had the answers to her questions.

Brooke's husband, though, was not amused by the idea. "Dear Lord," Brooke prayed, "if this is indeed an answer to prayer, please soften my husband's heart and help him understand the importance of this reunion. If this call was just a coincidence, please close the matter before it causes further harm to our marriage. Help me understand Your will. Through Christ, amen."

Three months after Brooke's sleepless night, she met with her ex-fiancé. As difficult as it was, all her questions were finally answered. Brooke gave him the letter she had written during the night in July, and that chapter of her life was closed with feelings of friendship and forgiveness. For the first time in her married life, she was able to make positive actions toward building a better relationship with her husband. The Lord was able to bring healing as a result of Brooke's trust in Him.

Dear heavenly Father,

Thank You for the privilege of prayer and for Your concern for me, especially when I suffer. Help me to always trust in You for guidance and healing. Your ways and timing are always perfect.

In Jesus' name I pray, amen.

Memory verse: Psalm 147:3
He heals the brokenhearted and binds up their wounds.

1. Several years ago, in what did Brooke put her trust? What happened as a result?

2. What main issue brought Brooke to the Lord in prayer?

3. What specific steps did she take towards healing?

4. What did the Lord do to answer Brooke's prayers?

5. Write about a time when you put your trust in the wrong thing. What happened as a result?

6. Now write about a specific prayer that God answered when you put your trust in Him.

7. What is trust?

8. Do you feel in your heart that you trust the Lord to control your life?

9. Can you think of any areas where complete trust in Him might be lacking in your life?

10. What do the following verses teach us about trust?

Psalm 26:1

Psalm 37:3

Psalm 125:1

Proverbs 3:5

Isaiah 26:4

11. When should we trust in the Lord?

Psalm 56:3

Psalm 62:8

12. What rewards do we receive when we trust in God?

Psalm 22:5

Psalm 28:7

Proverbs 16:20

Proverbs 28:25

Proverbs 29:25

Isaiah 28:16

Jeremiah 39:17, 18

Romans 10:11

1 Peter 2:6

13. What kind of trust can be deceiving?

Psalm 41:9

Psalm 52:7

Psalm 146:3

Micah 7:5

14. What happens when we trust in men or in anything other than God?

Proverbs 11:28

Proverbs 28:26

Jeremiah 17:5

15. Whom did Jesus heal according to the following verses?

Mark 1:34

Mark 6:56

Luke 9:11

16. What was the key to healing, according to Jesus, in the following passages of Scripture?

Mark 5:34

Luke 8:48

Luke 18:42

17. 1 Peter 2:24 tells us that "by His _____ you have been _____."

18. In what three ways can Christ heal us?

READ: John 9:1-34.
19. What specific instructions did Christ give to the blind man in order to receive healing (John 9:7)?

20. Explain what the blind man did as a result of his faith and belief in Jesus (give Scripture references).

21. What happened to the blind man as a result of his obedience (give references)?

22. How did the outsiders accept Jesus' healing of the blind man? Give the verses and a brief explanation.

23. How does John 9:35-41 parallel spiritual blindness and physical blindness?

24. Who are you most like in this story?

_____ The blind man—believing, trusting, and obedient.
_____ The Pharisees—doubtful and full of judgment.

25. Have you obeyed Christ's command to "go wash" in the watery grave of baptism to receive perfect healing from above?

26. Have you been washed, but now doubt?

SPIRITUAL CHALLENGE: Seek the Lord and trust Him completely for healing of all kinds: physical, spiritual, or emotional. If you are faithful and trust Him with all of your grievances and your life, He is just and will heal all of your infirmities. His rewards are wonderful when we fully trust in Him.

Chapter Thirteen

But Lord, I...I...I...

Mrs. Hill was filled with horror on judgment day when the Lord looked into her eyes and said, "Depart from me. I know you not."

Mrs. Hill was determined to see heaven and spend eternity there regardless of what the Bible said. She begged and pleaded with the Lord saying, "But I supported numerous charities and gave often to the poor. I volunteered many hours to various organizations and auxiliaries. I was a faithful wife to my husband for forty-five years and tender to my children. I never drank or participated in immoral activities. And I never murdered or stole anything from my neighbor. Don't You understand, Lord? I was a good, decent person. Please, please let me in."

As Mrs. Hill desperately pleaded her case before the Lord, she failed to remember that whenever someone approached her concerning God, the Bible, or His plan of salvation, she snubbed them with sarcasm. "I'm already good," she would say. "I don't need a crutch like some people. Besides, the church is full of hypocrites. Only the weak need a Savior."

Poor Mrs. Hill. She was indeed a beautiful and kind lady, but when she faced the most critical and important moment of her existence, she failed the test. She did not seek the Lord or listen to those who tried to reach her spiritually. She had not been washed in the blood of the Lamb. Her sins were not clean through faith in Christ, and she had not chosen to accept God's gracious gift of salvation.

Weeping and sobbing, she knelt down before Him and confessed that Jesus Christ is indeed Lord of lords and King of kings, but for Mrs. Hill it was too late.

Dear heavenly Father,

Help me to be alert to the fact that we will all ultimately acknowledge and bow down before You. Whether it is now or on judgment day, help me realize that the ultimate choice is up to me. Give me the strength to make the wisest decision and not depart from it.

In Jesus' name I pray, amen.

Memory Verse: Romans 2:13

For it is not those who hear the law who are righteous in God's sight, but it is those who obey the law who will be declared righteous.

1. Why did Mrs. Hill consider herself to be a good, moral person?

2. How did Mrs. Hill respond when others tried to share the gospel message with her?

3. What kinds of sarcastic remarks did she make in reference to Christ and/or Christians?

4. Do you think Mrs. Hill was originally afraid to die? Explain your answer.

5. What was Mrs. Hill expecting would get her into heaven?

6. Give the definition of "obedience."

7. What is important to God?

John 13:15-17

1 Corinthians 7:19

8. According to the following Scriptures, what did Jesus teach concerning our walk with Him and our reward of eternal life?

John 8:51

John 14:15

John 14:23

John 15:10

9. Who is righteous in God's sight?

Romans 2:13

10. Who will enter heaven?

Matthew 5:20

Matthew 7:21

11. How does Jesus judge our love for Him (John 14:24)?

12. What did the Spirit-led apostle Paul teach in Philippians 4:9?

READ: Matthew 7:24-29.
13. What must we do to be like the wise man?

14. To what was Jesus referring when He spoke of "the rock"?

15. Who is the foolish man?

16. What valuable information can we glean from the Old Testament in reference to obedience?

Deuteronomy 5:9

Deuteronomy 5:29

Deuteronomy 29:9

Deuteronomy 30:15, 16

Job 36:11

17.How can we have spiritual assurance that God is with us?

1 John 2:17

1 John 3:23

SPIRITUAL CHALLENGE: What will Jesus say to you on judgment day? Will He be more likely to say, "Well done, thou good and faithful servant," or "Depart from me. I never knew you"?

Romans 14:10-12 tells us that on judgment day each of us will give an account of himself or herself to God. We are indeed accountable to God for our own lives and for the choices we make.

If you are not a Christian, but would like to obey God and become one of His children, please don't wait any longer. Satan wants nothing more than for you to die in your sinful state. For Mrs. Hill it was too late. What will it be for you?

If you are a Christian, but need to obey the Lord concerning some of His other commands or teachings discussed in previous lessons, why not begin today? Each of Christ's commands is vitally important, and we have no assurance of tomorrow. Jesus may very well return tonight.

Appendix

The Lord's Perfect Plan for Salvation

Before you begin, I encourage you to pray to God, in Jesus' name (John 15:16 and Colossians 3:17), for wisdom and guidance. Don't be afraid to ask Him for an open heart and a clear mind.

I have spent many hours studying the Scriptures and the biblical plan of salvation. Several of the Bible references are written out to aid those of you who might not have a Bible. If you do have a Bible, please use it as you study.

On this _____ day of _____, I earnestly searched the Scriptures and studied out the Lord's plan of salvation.

_____
(your signature)

Who is God?

God is our heavenly Father and the creator of all things.

"In the beginning God created the heavens and the earth" (Genesis 1:1).

"So God created man in his own image, in the image of God he created him; male and female he created them" (Genesis 1:27).

"God saw all that he had made, and it was very good" (Genesis 1:31a).

Who is Jesus?

Jesus is the Son of God.

While Jesus was on earth, God spoke from heaven and said *"You are my Son, whom I love; with you I am well pleased"* (Mark 1:11b).

Where did Jesus originate?

"In the beginning was the Word, and the Word was with God, and the Word was God. The word became flesh and made his dwelling among us" (John 1:1, 14).

Jesus was the Word who was with God when all things were created. When the time was right God sent His Son, Who became flesh and lived on the earth.

Why did Jesus come to earth?

Jesus came to earth as God's sacrificial lamb to take away the sins of the world (John 1:29). He was tempted and tried just as you and I are; only He remained perfect and holy unto death.

"He committed no sin, and no deceit was found in his mouth. When they hurled their insults at him, he did not retaliate; when he suffered, he made no threats. Instead, he entrusted himself to him who judges justly. He himself bore our sins in his body on the tree, so that we might die to sins and live for righteousness; by his wounds you have been healed" (1 Peter 2:22-24).

Why was Jesus willing to suffer and die?

Jesus was willing to sacrifice Himself because He loves us and He was obedient to God, His Father. Jesus said, *"My command is this: Love each other as I have loved you. Greater love has no one than this, that he lay down his life for his friends. You are my friends if you do what I command"* (John 15:12-14).

Jesus also said, *"The world must learn that I love the Father and that I do exactly what my Father has commanded me"* (John 14:31; see also Romans 5:6-8).

Jesus was in great tribulation knowing He would soon be crucified. Shortly before soldiers came and seized Him, He knelt down and prayed, *"Father, if you are willing, take this cup from me; yet not my will, but yours be done"* (Luke 22:42).

"He was oppressed and afflicted, yet he did not open his mouth; he was led like a lamb to the slaughter" (Isaiah 53:7a).

Jesus obeyed God unto death—cruel death on a cross—and, as a result, He overcame the power of sin and death so that we can be saved from eternal punishment. But we must also obey God unto death, just as Jesus did (Luke 9:62).

Why is there a separation between us and God?

We are separated from God because of our sins.

What is sin?

Sin is a transgression of God's law. *"Everyone who sins breaks the law; in fact, sin is lawlessness"* (1 John 3:4).

Who has sinned?

Romans 3:23 says, *"for all have sinned and fall short of the glory of God."*

"We all, like sheep, have gone astray, each of us has turned to his own way; and the Lord has laid on him [Jesus] the iniquity of us all" (Isaiah 53:6).

Jesus had the power to send that mocking crowd at His crucifixion straight to hell, and He has the power to do so to us as well, but He didn't. Instead, out of love and obedience, He shed His blood and died for us.

Is hell a real place?

Yes, the Bible clearly warns us about hell. It tells us that hell is a *"lake of fire"* (Revelation 20:14). In Matthew 13:40-42, Jesus refers to hell as *"the fiery furnace, where there will be weeping and gnashing of teeth,"* and in Matthew 25:41 He describes hell as *"the eternal fire prepared for the devil and his angels."*

Who saves us from our sins, hell, and spiritual death?

Only God can save us. We cannot save ourselves. *"For it is by [God's] grace you have been saved, through faith—and this not from yourselves, it is the gift of God—not by works, so that no one can boast. For we are God's workmanship, created in Christ Jesus to do good works, which God prepared in advance for us to do"* (Ephesians 2:8-10).

Romans 6:23 says, *"For the wages of sin is death, but the gift of God is eternal life in Christ Jesus our Lord."*

Who does God want to be saved?

"God our Savior, wants all men to be saved and come to the knowledge of truth" (1 Timothy 2:3, 4, RSV).

"The Lord is not slow in keeping his promise, as some understand slowness. He is patient with you, not wanting anyone to perish, but everyone to come to repentance" (2 Peter 3:9).

Does the Old Testament have any value for us who live under the New Testament today?

Yes, the Old Testament is very important to understand. It is a part of God's inspired Word, and gives us the history of God's dealing with man from the very beginning. It deals with such important matters as the entrance of sin into the world and God's covenant with Abraham to send Jesus. It tells of the Law of Moses, given to the Jews as a tutor to bring them to Christ (Galatians 3). *But we do not live under the Old Testament today!* God sent His Son Jesus as our Savior and He fulfilled the covenant with Abraham, as well as the Law and the prophets. The old law was *cancelled* by being *nailed to the cross* (Colossians 2:14). We live under the New Testament—a new and better covenant with better promises than the Old. Unlike the people of the Old Testamet, Chrisitans enjoy the greatest possible earthly relationship with God—one that He planned for the church from the beginning (Ephesians 3:10, 11). We are *God's children*, forgiven here and now. The best claim that could be made under the old law was that of being the *children of Abraham* or the *children of Israel*.

Faith and obedience have always been required by God. In the Old Testament, God told Noah to build an ark in a land where it had never rained. He told Noah it would save him and his family from the flood God was going to send to the entire earth. God gave Noah specific instructions on how to build the ark and what to take on it.

"Noah did everything just as God commanded him" (Genesis 6:22).

As a result, Noah, his wife, his sons, and their wives were saved from destruction (the flood). Noah obeyed God to the exact measure.

In another Old Testament story, God told Abraham, *"Take your son, your only son, Isaac, whom you love, and go to the region of Moriah. Sacrifice him there as a burnt offering on one of the mountains I will tell you about"* (Genesis 22:2). Abraham was probably very sad and upset when God requested him to sacrifice Isaac, but he did not argue with God or question Him. Instead, he remained faithful.

"Early the next morning Abraham got up and saddled his donkey. He took with him two of his servants and his son Isaac. When he had cut enough wood for the burnt offering, he set out for the place God had told him about" (Genesis 22:3). *"When they reached the place God had told him about, Abraham built an altar there and arranged the wood on it. He bound his son Isaac and laid him on the altar, on top of the wood. Then he reached out his hand and took the knife to slay his son. But the angel of the Lord called out to him from heaven, 'Abraham! Abraham!' 'Here I am,' he replied. 'Do not lay a hand on the boy,' he said. 'Do not do anything to him. Now I know that you fear God, because you have not withheld from me your son, your only son'"* (Genesis 22:9-12). Abraham obeyed the Lord, and his son was allowed to live. Both Noah and Abraham demonstrated a tremendous amount of faith when their belief in God turned to obedience.

As in the days of Noah and Abraham, God also tests our faith today to see if we really love Him. Before we continue, we need to understand what faith is. As in the examples above, *faith* is a general term which requires both believing and obeying. What would have happened to Noah if he had told God, "I believe You will send a flood, but I don't think it is necessary to build an ark" (see Hebrews 11:7). Would Noah have been saved? No, it was Noah's faith (belief and obedience) in God and His plan that saved him from perishing.

Will believing without obedience save us? James 2:19 says, *"You believe that there is one God. Good! Even the demons believe that—and shudder."* The demons believe, but they are not saved. Why? Because we are saved by faith, and faith requires both belief and obedience. If we have one and not the other, then we do not have faith. Let's look at James 2:26, *"As the body without the spirit is dead, so faith without deeds is dead."*

Romans 2:13 says, *"For it is not those who hear the law who are righteous in God's sight, but it is those who obey the law who will be declared righteous."* And Jesus said, *"If anyone loves me, he will obey my teaching. He who does not love me will not obey my teaching. These words you hear are not my own; they belong to the Father who sent me"* (John 14:23a, 24).

By the grace of God we can all be saved—through faith (belief and obedience). God's will shows that our belief in Him must be accompanied by obedience if we are to please Him. Once we hear the Word and believe in God and that Jesus Christ is His Son, and we realize our sinfulness, Scripture tells us that we must repent of our sins.

What does repent mean?

Repent means to be sorry and turn away from our transgressions (sinful or ungodly ways).

"Repent then, and turn to God, so that your sins may be wiped out, that times of refreshing may come from the Lord." (Acts 3:19).

Because Jesus humbled Himself unto death for us, God requires us to confess that Jesus is Lord. *"That if you confess with your mouth, 'Jesus is Lord,' and believe in your heart that God raised him from the dead, you will be saved"* (Romans 10:9).

There is one more commandment God and Jesus require for salvation.

Scripture tells us that we must be baptized. Before Jesus ascended into heaven, He left us with vital instructions. His final words—His last words spoken on this earth, at a time we would remember them most—were, *"All authority in heaven and on earth has been given to me. Therefore go and make disciples of all nations, baptizing them in the name of the Father and of the Son and of the Holy Spirit, and teaching them to obey everything that I have commanded you. And surely I am with you always, to the very end of the age"* (Matthew 28:18-20).

Mark 16:16 says, *"Whoever believes and is baptized will be saved, but whoever does not believe will be condemned."*

Is baptism really necessary for salvation?
Someone once told me, "I feel that I am a saved Christian, but I have never been baptized."

Since Jesus commanded baptism, it should never be an issue of debate. Unfortunately, Bible baptism is one of the most balked-at biblical teachings in today's religious society. Because of that, I would like to encourage every person who loves the Lord, or desires to become a Christian, to make it a priority to study baptism and the important role it plays in our salvation. Before we study its importance, however, we need to understand what it is.

The Bible speaks about several different baptisms, and when I studied them in detail I learned and understood the Bible even more clearly. To study them all would be a whole lesson it itself, so for now I would like to concentrate on the original baptism—the one baptism that relates to the forgiveness of one's sins—the one the apostle Paul referred to more than twenty years after the church began (in the book of Acts). In Ephesians 4:4, 5 Paul wrote, "There is one body and one Spirit—just as you were called to one hope when you were called—one Lord, one faith, one baptism."

The only baptism we can still practice today is the original water baptism.

What is water baptism according to Scripture?
The Bible makes it very clear that God's (water) baptism requires going down into the water and coming up out of the water (Acts 8:38, 39). There was always "much water." The original biblical Greek word for baptism is *baptizo*, which means immerse, dip, plunge, emerge, or submerge. When I looked at immerse, dip, plunge, emerge, and submerge in my common dictionary, I learned that those words mean to put something under an enveloping medium, to cover with water, to bury, to arise out of an unfortunate state, to plunge under, and to baptize.

There are other Greek words for *pour* or *sprinkle*. Those are *cheo* (to pour) and *rantizo* (to sprinkle). Water baptism is an immersion.

What is the purpose of water baptism and why is it so important?
In the book of Acts, when the Lord's church was first being established, we learn that belief and baptism went hand in hand.

Because of its importance, new converts to Christianity were baptized (immersed) immediately upon believing the gospel message, because this was when their sins were forgiven. Once their sins were washed away, they received the gift of the indwelling Holy Spirit. Let's look now at a few of the biblical accounts provided for us in the book of Acts.

"Peter replied, 'Repent and be baptized, every one of you, in the name of Jesus Christ for the forgiveness of your sins. And you will receive the gift of the Holy Spirit'" (Acts 2:38).

"Those who accepted his message were baptized, and about three thousand were added to their number that day" (Acts 2:41)

Paul (Saul) was baptized after having the gospel preached by Ananias to "wash your [his] sins away, calling on his [Jesus'] name." The Ethiopian eunuch saw the importance of baptism and was baptized along the roadside as soon as he found much water (Acts 8:26-39). The jailer and his family were also baptized immediately upon believing in the Lord Jesus, even though it was the middle of the night (Acts 16:25-34).

As we proceed through Scripture, we learn even more about the purpose of baptism. When we study the parable of the wedding banquet in Matthew 22:1-14, we are warned that (1) the day is coming when God no longer keeps inviting those who refuse Him; and (2) those who do come to Him must be clothed properly and on God's terms or they will be thrown out into outer darkness where there will be weeping and gnashing of teeth.

Galatians 3:26, 27 tells us that baptism clothes us with Christ. *"You are all sons of God through faith [belief and obedience] in Christ Jesus, for all of you who were baptized into Christ have clothed yourselves with Christ."*

Obeying the gospel message proclaims the death, burial, and resurrection of Jesus.

As Christians, the Bible tells us that we are to imitate Christ Jesus.

In 1 Peter 2:21 we read, *"To this you were called, because Christ suffered for you, leaving you an example, that you should follow in his steps."*

1 John 2:6 says, *"Whoever claims to live in him must walk as Jesus did."* Jesus lived, died on the cross (was crucified), was buried, rose from the dead, stayed on earth a little while longer, and then

ascended into heaven. We are to live, die to our sins (be crucified with Christ) by being buried in baptism, rise to walk the new life on earth, remain faithful, and someday go to heaven to be with God forever. The Bible says that baptism is a "burial." When something is buried, it is put underground. When we are spiritually buried with Christ, we are put under water (immersed).

The Bible asks, *"Or don't you know that all of us who were baptized into Christ Jesus were baptized into his death? We were therefore buried with him through baptism into death in order that, just as Christ was raised from the dead through the glory of the Father, we too may live a new life.*

"If we have been united with him like this in his death, we will certainly also be united with him in his resurrection. For we know that our old self was crucified with him so that the body of sin might be done away with, that we should no longer be slaves to sin—because anyone who has died has been freed from sin.

"Now if we died with Christ, we believe that we will also live with him. For we know that since Christ was raised from the dead, he cannot die again; death no longer has mastery over him. The death he died, he died to sin once for all; but the life he lives, he lives to God. In the same way, count yourselves dead to sin but alive to God in Christ Jesus" (Romans 6:3-11).

"Those who belong to Christ Jesus have crucified the sinful nature with its passions and desires" (Galatians 5:24).

Before Jesus died, Nicodemus was confused. *"'How can a man be born when he is old?' Nicodemus asked. 'Surely he cannot enter a second time into his mother's womb to be born!' Jesus answered, 'I tell you the truth, no one can enter the kingdom of God unless he is born of water and the Spirit. Flesh gives birth to flesh, but the Spirit gives birth to spirit'"* (John 3:4-6). Jesus told this already religious man that he must be born again.

Baptism gives us new birth. 1 Peter 1:22, 23 says, *"Now that you have purified yourselves by obeying the truth so that you have sincere love for your brothers, love one another deeply, from the heart. For you have been born again, not of perishable seed, but of imperishable, through the living and enduring word of God."*

Long ago, when God waited patiently in the days of Noah and the ark was being built, men continued to sin.

"In it [the ark] only a few people, eight in all, were saved through water, and this water symbolizes baptism that now saves you also—not the removal of dirt from the body but the pledge of a good conscience toward God" (1 Peter 3:20b, 21).

From the biblical references discussed above, we have obtained valuable information. We can easily conclude that water baptism was commanded by Jesus, His Spirit-filled apostles taught water baptism by immersion, and new converts to Christianity were baptized immediately upon believing. We also discovered that the first-century Christians realized that they had not obtained salvation (i.e., been forgiven of their sins, had their sins washed away, been added to the church) until they had been buried with their Lord in baptism.

We also learned from Scripture that baptism clothes us with Christ. Water baptism is a burial as well as a new birth (new life). This simple act of obedience also gives us the privilege of a clear conscience towards God, forgiveness of sins, and the gift of the Holy Spirit. There is nothing special about the water, but there are many special things about God's grace and the miracle He performs in forgiving us when we obey Him.

If God's baptism requires much water, then where did infant sprinkling come from?

Infant sprinkling was introduced as an invention of men—not God—basically for convenience, several hundred years after the death and resurrection of Jesus Christ. Jesus did not teach or command it. He Himself (our divine example) demonstrated the method, having been immersed in the Jordan River. He was perfect, so He was not baptized because He was a sinner, but rather the Bible says He was baptized "to fulfill all righteousness." As soon as Jesus was baptized, He went up out of the water. At that moment heaven was opened, and the Spirit of God descended like a dove and lighted upon Him. A voice from heaven said, *"This is my Son, whom I love; with him I am well pleased"* (Matthew 3:17).

Will small children go to hell if they die but are not sprinkled?

Like all other questions, let me answer this based on biblical facts. God is the "only and final judge," and His judgment is just. We are saved by faith (belief and obedience). *"Consequently, faith*

114

comes from hearing the message, and the message is heard through the word of Christ" (Romans 10:17). In each biblical account, people who wanted salvation were:

(1)   Old enough to understand what sin is and Who God is.

(2)   Old enough to repent of their sins and confess Jesus as Lord.

(3)   Old enough to willingly obey God and His instructions for salvation, and then to live a new life in Christ.

Innocent little babies and small children are not capable of doing these things. When children start feeling guilty for their mistakes, they become accountable and must choose which direction they want for their lives. Christianity is a choice.

Romans 14:12 tells us that "each of us will give an account of himself to God."

Jesus said, "Let the little children come to me, and do not hinder them, for the kingdom of God belongs to such as these" (Mark 10:14).

As a matter of fact, He even wants adults to become like children, receiving Him with humble and loving trust. "I tell you the truth, anyone who will not receive the kingdom of God like a little child will never enter it" (Mark 10:15).

Is sprinkling mentioned anywhere in the Bible?

Yes, it is. The Old Testament teaches us about sprinkling not only for sin offerings, but for other spiritual offerings as well (see the book of Leviticus for examples). There was one vital difference, however—animal blood was always used, not water. "In fact, the law requires that nearly everything be cleansed with blood, and without the shedding of blood there is no forgiveness" (Hebrews 9:22). New Testament Scriptures always refer to Christ's blood (see 1 Peter 1:2) since His blood replaced all animal sacrifices from the Old Testament. Hebrews 10:22 says, "Having our hearts sprinkled to cleanse us from a guilty conscience and having our bodies washed with pure water."

When we submit to baptism and are immersed into Christ, we contact the blood of Christ. Our bodies are washed with pure water, and the Lord cleanses our hearts.

Why is there so much conflict between religious groups over God's Word (the Holy Bible), and why do people believe in so many different ways of salvation? Have God's original teachings for salvation changed over the years?

No, God's teachings for salvation have not changed over the years. Unfortunately, even in the time period shortly after Christ died, there was quarreling among the Christians. *"One of you says, 'I follow Paul'; another, 'I follow Apollos'; another, 'I follow Cephas'; still another, 'I follow Christ.' Is Christ divided?"* (1 Corinthians 1:12b, 13a).

In Galatians 1:6-10, the apostle Paul, sent not by men but by God, was upset with false teachers who were coming in and upsetting his work of truth.

We must realize that Jesus built one church, and one church only. Men have built many churches. The Bible tells us in Acts 5:29 that *"We must obey God rather than men!"*

Hebrews 12:2a says *"Let us fix our eyes on Jesus, the author and perfecter of our faith."*

The Bible also warns us in 2 Timothy 4:3, 4, *"For the time will come when men will not put up with sound doctrine. Instead, to suit their own desires, they will gather around them a great number of teachers to say what their itching ears want to hear. They will turn their ears away from the truth and turn aside to myths."*

This is happening now. Please don't get caught in the devil's trap! Twisted Scriptures, cults, and counterfeit teachings surround us and, sadly, look so authentic. Many people feel saved, but unfortunately feelings can be deceiving. The Bible says Satan is the father of lies (see John 8:42-47). A lie is a falsehood. God's plan for salvation is so beautiful and simple. Satan doesn't care how sincere or how spiritual we are. All he is concerned about is keeping us from being clothed with the blood of Christ, because if he succeeds at that we still belong to him! 2 Corinthians 11:14b, 15 warns us that *"Satan himself masquerades as an angel of light. It is not surprising, then, if his servants masquerade as servants of righteousness."*

"Dear friends, do not believe every spirit, but test the spirits to see whether they are from God, because many false prophets have gone out into the world" (1 John 4:1). For further study, see also Matthew 7:21-23 and Galatians 1:6-9.

Jesus said, *"Blessed are those who wash their robes, that they may have the right to the tree of life and may go through the gates into the city. Outside are the dogs, those who practice magic arts, the sexually immoral, the murderers, the idolaters and everyone who loves and practices falsehood"* (Revelation 22:14, 15).

It is important for us to remember that God is God. The Lord is not impressed with man's opinions, and He is angered by false teachings.

"There is a way that seems right to a man, but in the end it leads to [spiritual] death" (Proverbs 14:12).

John the Baptist prepared the way (Matthew 3:1-6). Jesus demonstrated the way (Matthew 3:16, 17). And Jesus said, *"I am the way and the truth and the life. No one comes to the Father except through me"* (John 14:6).

Many people sincerely love the Lord, but are sincerely misled. Paul (Saul) was, but when he learned the truth, he obeyed. The whole purpose of this life is to obey and serve the Lord. He did so much for us. As believers in Christ, we need to be united. Satan loves nothing more than spiritual weakness and division. The word *Christian* bears great responsibilities, and those who claim it need to adhere closely to the doctrines of our precious Lord and Savior, Jesus Christ. The desire and goal of every Christian should be to imitate Christ and then stand firm, in all circumstances, with unwavering faith, for what is right and true.

God loves each one of us, but He will never force us to love and obey Him. He has given us a free will. If we refuse to completely obey the teachings that God created and Jesus taught, then we are saying no to God and yes to Satan and hell.

I am sharing this, not to upset or confuse you, but because I love you and care about your soul. These things are not based on my opinions or on man's rules, but rather on the unchanging Word of God.

Once we learn God's truth, the Lord wants us to *"Do everything without complaining or arguing, so that you may become blameless and pure, children of God without fault in a crooked and depraved generation"* (Philippians 2:14, 15a), and to *"Repent and be baptized, every one of you, in the name of Jesus Christ for the forgiveness of your sins. And you will receive the gift of the Holy Spirit"* (Acts 2:38).

Do you need to set a date when you want to be saved?

No.

"I tell you, now is the time of God's favor, now is the day of salvation" (2 Corinthians 6:2b).

Please don't wait. It is too risky to hold out until we get that new home or car, our own business, our next college degree, or whatever else it is that holds us back from obeying God. James 4:14 says, *"Why, you do not even know what will happen tomorrow. What is your life? You are a mist that appears for a little while and then vanishes."*

I urge you to be very careful. Nothing is as important as eternal life. Once we die, it is too late. Jesus is coming back to take His people home to live with Him for eternity. Will you be ready to meet Him when He calls your name?

"'Come now, let us reason together,' says the Lord. 'Though your sins are like scarlet, they shall be as white as snow; though they are red as crimson, they shall be like wool. If you are willing and obedient, you will eat the best from the land; but if you resist and rebel, you will be devoured by the sword.' For the mouth of the Lord has spoken" (Isaiah 1:18-20).

When we obey God's plan of salvation, including baptism by immersion, we are not doing anything to earn our salvation. We are simply accepting the Lord, His love, His grace, His forgiveness, and His special gift to us, the Holy Spirit. We are saved because God is good—not because we are good. Belief and obedience mark only the beginning of our walk with Christ. Christianity is a lifelong commitment. The old must pass, and we must remain faithful and obedient to God and His ways all the days of our lives (see Revelation 2:10). Christianity also means that we are heirs of a wonderful God. It means salvation, eternal life, happiness, and joy. Don't miss out on the hope of eternal life in heaven with our Lord.

"The Lord is compassionate and gracious, slow to anger, abounding in love. He will not always accuse, nor will he harbor his anger forever; he does not treat us as our sins deserve or repay us according to our iniquities. For as high as the heavens are above the earth, so great is his love for those who fear him; as far as the east is from the west, so far has he removed our transgressions from us. As a father has compassion on his children, so the Lord has compassion on those who fear him; for he knows how we are formed, he remembers that we are dust. As for man,

his days are like grass, he flourishes like a flower of the field; the wind blows over it and it is gone, and its place remembers it no more. But from everlasting to everlasting the Lord's love is with those who fear him, and his righteousness with their children's children—with those who keep his covenant and remember to obey his precepts. The Lord has established his throne in heaven, and his kingdom rules over all. Praise the Lord, you his angels, you mighty ones who do his bidding, who obey his word. Praise the Lord, all his heavenly hosts, you his servants who do his will. Praise the Lord, all his works everywhere in his dominion. Praise the Lord, O my soul" (Psalm 103:8-22).